Lectionary Stories *for* Preaching *and* Teaching

Lent and Easter Seasons Edition Cycle A

for the Revised Common Lectionary

A Compendium of Stories from
StoryShare
a Component of **SermonSuite.com**
from CSS Publishing Company

CSS Publishing Company, Inc.
Lima, Ohio

LECTIONARY STORIES FOR PREACHING AND TEACHING
LENT / EASTER SEASONS EDITION, CYCLE A

FIRST EDITION
Copyright © 2013
by CSS Publishing Co., Inc.

Published by CSS Publishing Company, Inc., Lima, Ohio 45807. All rights reserved. No part of this publication may be reproduced in any manner whatsoever without the prior permission of the publisher, except in the case of brief quotations embodied in critical articles and reviews. Inquiries should be addressed to: CSS Publishing Company, Inc., Permissions Department, 5450 N. Dixie Highway, Lima, Ohio 45807.

For more information about CSS Publishing Company resources, visit our website at www.csspub.com, email us at csr@csspub.com or call (800) 241-4056.

ISBN-13: 978-0-7880-2748-2
ISBN-10: 0-7880-2748-4   PRINTED IN USA

Table of Contents

Introduction	5
Ash Wednesday *Joel 2:1-2, 12-17* The Terrible Dark Day	7
Lent 1 *Genesis 2:15-17; 3:1-7* It's Not My Fault	10
Lent 2 *John 3:1-17* Three Field Goals and a Touchdown	12
Lent 3 *Romans 5:1-11* The Account	16
Lent 4 *John 9:1-41* The Disturbing Witness of Grace	21
Lent 5 *Ezekiel 37:1-14* Bones	24
Passion / Palm Sunday *Matthew 26:14—27:66* Is It Truth?	28
Maundy Thursday *1 Corinthians 11:23-26* Do This Remembering Me...	31
Good Friday *Isaiah 52:13—53:12* Reflecting Martyrs	33

Easter Sunday 37
Acts 10:34-43; Colossians 3:1-4
Anticipation

Easter 2 40
John 20:19-31
Tracks

Easter 3 44
Acts 2:14a, 22-32
Speak the Truth in Love

Easter 4 49
Psalm 23
Familiar Words

Easter 5 51
John 14:1-14
Please Don't Forget Me

Easter 6 54
Acts 17:22-31
Looking for God

Ascension of Our Lord 56
Acts 1:1-11
Wayne's Deployment

Easter 7 59
John 17:1-11
Where's the Finish Line?

About the Authors 64

Introduction

Since you are reading this, you probably preach on a regular basis. It is important to not only bring God's word to the members of your congregation but to help make the gospel of Christ engaging and thought-provoking.

Most people know that Jesus, the Master Storyteller, very often used stories and parables to make an important point to his listeners about God's kingdom. Following his example, we know that helping people to understand God's word through the telling of a story not only provides additional interest in a message, but also makes that same message easier to understand.

Over the years, CSS has published thousands of relevant, interesting, and inspiring anecdotes and stories to season a pastor's sermon. Not only has CSS produced numerous books to aid pastors in this important part of ministry but CSS also has a weekly online service called **StoryShare**, a component of **SermonSuite.com**, that was created to bring preachers the most timely and relevant illustrations possible. This edition of stories and anecdotes, gleaned from **StoryShare** for Cycle A, are written to dovetail with the readings from the Revised Common Lectionary and will serve you well as extended illustrations or in many cases, stand-alone sermons.

It is our hope that the stories in this book will not only assist you, the pastor, in your preaching but will also help you throughout your ministry.

The editors at CSS Publishing Company, Inc.

Ash Wednesday
Joel 2:1-2, 12-17
by Peter Andrew Smith

The Terrible Dark Day

Carried by the wind, a small pod covered with spikes fell onto a field. The precious seeds within spilled into the ground and after the rains fell, one of them sprouted and took root. A tiny shoot pushed up through the ground and reached toward the light. The shoot grew into a sapling, which grew into a small tree.

As the tree's branches spread out, a bird flying past landed and took rest among its leaves. The bird flew on but soon other birds used the branches of the young tree as a resting place. One bird took shelter there from the elements and returned time and time again to the tree. As the tree grew larger the bird built a nest, attracted a mate, and soon the nest was filled with eggs. The eggs hatched and the baby birds used the branches of the tree as places to sing their songs and build their own nests.

As the seasons passed, the tree kept reaching toward the sun. The branches grew thicker and the trunk grew sturdy and strong. In the middle of the field, the tree stood tall and proud anchored firmly by deep roots that tightly gripped the earth.

When the time came, tiny pods covered with spikes containing precious seeds appeared on the branches of the tree. They started small, then grew, and when it was their time, they fell upon the ground. Each one of those pods landed under the shadow of the mighty tree with its full branches and towering height. Without the light of the sun and the kiss of the rain, the seeds never took root and simply rotted where they fell.

One season the tree stopped reaching for the sun. The branches did not extend any further and the roots did not seek any deeper. The birds that were there remained but no new ones came to the tree or near the field where the lone tree stood tall and full. The leaves still came each spring and fell each autumn. When it was time, the pods full of precious seeds developed and dropped from the tree but the seeds never went beyond the shadow of the tree and none of them ever sprouted.

The insects came seeking to eat away at the vitality of the tree as did the various diseases that sought to overcome its health. Each time the great branches, sturdy trunk, and the deep roots allowed the tree to resist. Yet, each time the tree took longer to heal itself following the assault of the forces looking to consume its life.

One season when the spiky pods had again sprouted on the tree, the sky grew dark during the day. As the light died, the birds stopped their songs, and huddled close to the trunk of the tree as an eerie silence covered the field. The calm was broken by the gentle rustle of the leaves. The gentle rustle grew to a roar as a persistent wind began to blow. The leaves shook and the birds hung on in the shelter of the many branches of the great tall tree. The persistent wind became a raging gale. Nests were pulled apart and scattered to the wind as eggs smashed into the ground and the birds were driven from their refuge.

The wind tore and bit into the tree pulling and tearing at it. Leaves were ripped in pieces and torn from the branches. The branches themselves strained under the fury of the wind. The smallest ones were twisted back and forth until they snapped off. The larger ones bent and strained under the relentless pressure.

The wind crashed and pounded against the tree with such

a terrible fury that the mighty trunk itself began to sway from side to side. The roots struggled to hold the tree in place as the wind slammed into the tree again and again. Then all at once the wind stopped.

The once-mighty tree stood broken and battered among the shattered nests and debris. The roots had only a fragile hold on the earth and sap dripped from cracks in the trunk. The branches hung twisted and warped, stripped bare of all but a leaf here and there. Only the memory of the tree's former majesty remained as the light returned and a gentle rain began to fall.

As the days passed, the tree began to grow new leaves and the branches spread out in the embrace of the light. The roots tightened their grip on the earth and then dug deeper into the ground. New branches grew in place of those which had been lost and the tree reached upward once again. The birds slowly returned to the branches. Nests and songs of life returned to the tree.

Beyond where the branches stretched, pods covered in spikes broke open and the seeds within fell into the embrace of the earth. The seeds took root and grew into saplings. The saplings pushed toward the light and as their branches reached out they grew strong and tall outside the shadow of the tree that had stood for so long by itself in the field. After the terrible dark day, the tree was no longer alone in the field. It stood in the middle of a new forest.

Lent 1
Genesis 2:15-17; 3:1-7
by C. David McKirachan

It's Not My Fault

Through the years one of the most frustrating exchanges I've had with my sons has always gone something like, "This room is wrecked" (that's me), "I didn't do it" (that is one of them). "Well, let's clean it up" (that's me), "I didn't make the mess, why should I have to clean it up?" (that's one of them). "I don't care who made the mess, it's got to get cleaned up" (that's an irate me). "That's not fair" (that is the philosophically whining them). "Right. Such is life" (that is the existentialist me). I kept waiting for them to grow into seeing and doing, into taking responsibility for having a nice living space. What they gave me on a consistent basis was an argument about whose fault the situation was.

They're not alone. Our justice system is big on measuring culpability. Our civil legal system is big on assigning blame. Our political system uses scapegoats to avoid responsibility and divert attention. Corporations are big at blame. Don't forget your paper trail. And then there's marriage and divorce. Almost never do we face a situation with the attitude, "Here's the mess we have — now let's get to it."

I think the biblical story of the fall demonstrates this so well. We're so ready to blame the snake. He just happens to be crafty. I think he does pretty well for a reptile with a weird tongue. No lisp recorded in my Bible. Then we blame Eve. I've heard so many jokes about Eve, most of them sexist. How would you like to be the mother of humanity? Talk about a setup. You'd be guilty for everything. Then there's Adam. Here come the cracks and jokes again. Good old Dad.

Can't get no respect.

Sin belongs to all of us. It doesn't matter who did the deed. We've got to live with the mess and do our best to clean it up — unless we want to remain children and continue driving our parent nuts. Okay, now we're down to it. It's hard to let go of the child thing. It feels like we're sheltered when we can argue with the parents, because it reminds us of the time when we weren't responsible for soup to nuts — the time when there was somebody in charge who could make sense of the whole thing.

The hardest part of losing my parents, other than missing them, was realizing that now I was an adult. Now, whether I whined or not, I was in charge of making things happen. No safety net. I think God wants us to grow up. When it comes down to it, it doesn't really matter whose fault it happens to be — we've still got the mess to clean up. Our brothers and sisters are in trouble and no matter how good or pure or wise we happen to be, it's all in the family.

Maybe we were thrown out of the garden because we became adolescents. Even God would have a hard time with a sixteen-year-old.

Lent 2
John 3:1-17
by John Smylie

Three Field Goals and a Touchdown

There were only two minutes left in the game. The home team called a timeout — they were behind by 16 points, but at this point it was a matter of pride. They knew they had very little chance of winning — they had been outplayed through most of the game but still they were fighting to score so as not to be shut out. The other team had already scored three field goals and a touchdown and an extra point. The team was not comfortable with 16-0 — they wanted to get something on the board.

"Come on boys," the coach said as his voice broke huddle on the sidelines as the boys prepared to walk back on to the field, "Let's not get shut out." It was evening, the sun was already below the horizon, and the last glimmers of sunshine tickled the clouds with pink light. The crowd was cheering the boys on, the band was beating on their drums from the sideline, the cheerleaders were shaking their pom-poms, and the boys went out onto the field. They were already on the opposing team's 30-yard line with two minutes left in the game. Their field-goal kicker had a range of about 40 yards and so the boys needed to move the ball at least seven more yards.

The boys lined up in a passing formation, the ball was hiked, and the quarterback pretended to throw the ball out to the right side of the field to his wide receiver and then tucked the ball under his arm and ran straight ahead. There was a slight hole in the middle of the line and he picked up four yards. Second down, another run, and three more yards and only 45 seconds left on the clock. Third down brought a quarterback sneak moving the ball a bit closer to the center of the field, one more yard gained. Fourth down, six seconds left on the clock, and the last time out used. The ball was now on the 22-yard line and when you add ten yards for the end zone and seven yards for the snap, the kicker was facing a 39-yard field goal right at the edge of his range.

In the stands there was a fan who had been holding up a sign all game long. The sign read — 3:16. Now the kicker, his name was Fred, was a member of an organization that involved Christian athletes and he knew what 3:16 meant. "For God so loved the world that he gave his only son, so that everyone who believes in him may not perish but may have eternal life." The kicker smiled to himself thinking that he had an opportunity to make the score 3-16.

It was fourth down, the ball on the 22-yard line, the snap was good — the hold was good — the kick was good — 3-16 was the final score. The crowd erupted even though their team had lost — the band played the school fight song — the cheerleaders screamed — the players held their heads a little higher as they greeted the opposing team.

It was quiet in the locker room as the boys showered and changed into their civilian clothes. The coach commended the boys on their final effort and said that he would see them on Monday when they came to practice. One of the boys whose name was Joe came up to the kicker and asked, "Did you see that guy in the stands holding a sign that said 3:16?"

"Yeah, I did. In fact when I saw it, it gave me some courage and confidence as I was getting ready to kick the ball."

"What do you mean? I thought the guy was kind of a nut, but now I wonder if he was some sort of prophet. How did he know the score would be 3-16?"

The kicker smiled and wondered if this might be the

deeper reason for the score being what it was. His teammate who was asking him about the gentleman in the stands and his 3:16 sign was a young man with a deeply troubled past. He'd been in one foster home after another. His parents had been drug addicts, caught up in the methamphetamine addiction pattern. It was amazing that he was doing as well as he was, but there was a very hard edge to him and he'd never been exposed to the gospel.

Fred the kicker said, "Let me tell you about that guy who was holding a sign, let me tell you where he got that score from. I'm heading over to a meeting now for the Fellowship of Christian athletes, why don't you come with me and I'll explain it to you."

"Sure, why not, I've got nothing else to do, sounds good," said Joe.

The boys got into a 1962 VW bug and headed over to the back of a coffee shop where the meeting was held. On the way, Fred explained to Joe what John 3:16 was. He described why it was so important to so many — and why he figured the man in the stands was holding up a placard with those numbers in bold print. Then he explained how that verse fit into the whole story. He told Joe how there was a rather well-known man named Nicodemus who was a leader among his people who came to Jesus by night. That was a big risk, Fred told Joe, because if Nicodemus had been seen by his own people he would have likely been rejected — seen as some sort of traitor to his faith.

Fred went on to tell Joe that it seemed like lots of folks even today were afraid to find out about Jesus. "You know Joe, you and I are kind of like Nicodemus tonight, we're going to a meeting in the back of a coffee shop, most everybody else on our team will be going out to parties, but you and I — well maybe we'll learn something tonight that will have real value for us for the rest of our lives. I'm kind of glad the score was 3-16. It's given me an opportunity to do something that I'm usually too chicken to do. Joe I'm not sure anybody on the team knows that I come to these Fellowship of Christian athletes meetings, but I'm glad you know and I hope you find what I find in them."

"Joe," Fred said, "I've usually been too embarrassed to invite anybody to the meetings, especially my teammates. I find myself nervous that I will be rejected by the team — you know we kickers often feel like we are on the edge of the whole team experience as it is — and so while the team goes off and does its thing I tend to gravitate to my church and small group — Joe thanks for coming with me tonight."

Joe was not used to being talked to this way. There was a deep hunger in him to be included somewhere, to be a part of something greater than himself. That was a big part of the reason of why he was on the football team, he wanted to be part of a group, part of something greater than himself, but he was disappointed that he hardly ever got to play. "Fred, I'd like to learn more about Nicodemus and I'm glad the score was 3-16, thanks for inviting me to the meeting tonight."

They drove in silence for a while and Fred thought to himself — I'm glad they made three field goals and a touchdown — and I sure am glad I made that kick at the end of the game. He marveled a bit at how these things came together because he had wanted to invite someone to join him at the Fellowship of Christian athletes for a while. Perhaps more than ever before he believed that God really did love the world, and God cared about him and Joe and that God would do anything to open the door to lead them to eternal life. He was glad for the journey that Nicodemus made those many years ago and he was glad for their own journey. All because of three field goals, a touchdown, and a 39-yard field goal with time expiring at the end of the game, there was rejoicing in heaven as well as on the sidelines and in the coffee shop!

Lent 3
Romans 5:1-11
by Keith Hewitt

The Account

"Will there be anything else?" the shopkeeper asked, as he finished wrapping the meat in white paper, then tied it tightly with white string that came from a spool that hung just overhead, above the top of the cooler.

The woman looked at the groceries gathered there — flour, check; eggs, check; sausage, check; ground beef, check — then glanced at her list, mentally scratched off a couple of items that were just too expensive; she had included them on a whim, hoping that they might be on sale at the little corner market. Jago sometimes did that, if he could catch something that was about to turn, but hadn't quite gone bad, yet. She shook her head. "That's it, thanks." Pause. "Can you put this on our account, please?"

"Sure thing," the man answered, almost at once. He wrote up a receipt, showed it to her, then stuck it on a spindle next to the cash register, along with a couple of dozen others. Later, he would go into his books and add the day's groceries to the tab they had running; she looked away, shocked once at how much she had spent, and again at how much she thought would be available to spend.

"Walter gets paid tomorrow, doesn't he?" the shopkeeper asked as he packed the groceries into a plain brown bag. He almost managed to sound casual.

She appeared to think for a moment, then nodded slightly. "Yes, yes he does. I'm surprised you remember."

He shrugged, rubbed a finger under his eye, bumping up his glasses. "You kind of have to these days. You've got to know who's not working, and who is — and when they get paid. You know —" He hesitated, then smiled shyly. "My wife gets nervous about all these accounts, and when they're going to get paid." He shrugged again, bumped his glasses, "I tell her, 'Don't worry so much, it's not good for you. Besides, now that Roosevelt is in, things are going to get better.'"

"I sure hope so," she said, and reached for the bag. "Thanks for your help — and your understanding."

He held the bag for the barest moment as she started to take it and looked at her through thick lenses that made his eyes seem huge. "We need to have something paid on your account," he said quietly, almost apologetically. "It's up past forty dollars, now."

She nodded again, sliding the bag across the counter, turning her eyes away. "Of course," she said. "Tomorrow, then." She cradled the bag in her arms and walked out the door, listened to the jingling bell that mocked her with its airy cheeriness as she pulled the door open. She walked down the couple of concrete steps to the sidewalk, rounded the corner, and hurried home, feet taking her on her way while her mind struggled with other things. $40? It had to be closer to $45, she calculated, trying to remember her last couple of purchases.

When was the last time they'd been able to pay down the account? She shook her head; the longer they went, the worse it got. They lived at the mercy of her husband's job, and there just hadn't been that many hours lately. He was a die maker, a good, solid job that a man ought to be able to raise a family on — but when the factory sat idle, there was no need for his skills.

She fretted about it the rest of the night — as she had so many other nights before — in silence that sat like a rock on her chest. She couldn't talk to him about it — he had other worries — and there was no talking to the children, of course. Although they must suspect — they must all suspect something, she thought. How thin could you make a stew, before it became soup — and how thin could you make the soup, before it became broth? But nobody ever said anything, sitting around the table.

She was waiting for her husband the next day when he came home from work. As he did each payday, he went to the Building & Loan to cash his check, and pay on their mortgage, returning with whatever was left over tucked away in a creased white envelope. It had been a better week than others she thought as he took the envelope out of his pocket — they ought to be able to knock some of the forty-plus dollars down. She thought about what they would do, what they could pay off, what they should keep for expenses....

Across the table, their daughters ate butter and sugar sandwiches, watching as the ritual played out.

He put his thumb under the flap, ripped it down the length of the envelope, and puffed it open, dumped out the contents on the pale yellow linoleum tablecloth. The bill slid out silently, the coins clinked softly, almost drowned out by the noise of the wind in the leaves outside the kitchen window. She stared at what was left of his pay, even as he lowered his head and turned away. Her fingers flashed out to the table, shaking slightly as she sorted through once, then again, to be sure. The answer was the same both times: $1.27.

The hope that had stirred for a moment — even as a part of her knew it was fantasy — sank, and sucked her soul down with it, a torpedoed ship that took dreams to the bottom where they would never see the light of day again. After what seemed like a long time, she realized the girls were still there — she looked at them, forced a smile, and said gently, "It's good. There's something left over this week."

And hated the lie.

Although Columbus Street ran along the crest of a hill, when she walked to the market after dinner it seemed like a steep, uphill journey. For a block, she spun possibilities in her mind, tops of flashing ideas that whirled and wobbled, then crashed on the hard floor of reality. She turned the corner in front of the market, stopped and looked in the window for a moment or two; there was nobody else in there. She mounted the steps, pulled open the door, and listened to the bell announce her presence.

The store smelled of fresh meat and despair, the floorboards beneath her creaked as she walked directly to the counter at the back of the store. Jago was there, sorting through the receipts on the spindle next to the cash register, transferring charges into an open ledger. He looked up and seemed surprised to see her. "Hello," he said, capping the fountain pen in his hand and closing the big book. "I wasn't expecting to see you again, so soon."

"I said I would be here," she reminded him. "Remember, Walter got paid today."

"I know, but —" he opened the ledger, ran a finger down the side of the page, as though to check something, then looked up again. "— I assumed you knew."

"Knew what?"

He put a hand over the names above hers, turned the book around so she could see it. "Your account — it was paid off this morning. A gentleman came in and asked about it, but it seemed like he already knew what the tab was. And then he paid it." He stabbed a fingertip at the balance column. "See: zero balance. You're paid in full."

Her heart was racing, wanted to fly out of her chest. "Who — who —?" she repeated, stumbling, unable to complete the thought.

"I don't know." He shrugged, bumped his glasses with his finger. "He seemed like a nice young man but never gave his name. He just said maybe you would find him some day — if you wanted to look for him." He closed the book again and peered at her with out-sized eyes. "Did you need anything else tonight?"

"No." She shook her head. "No, we're fine. Thank you." She retreated quickly from the store, afraid to linger, lest he discover it was some kind of mistake. As she walked home, steps clicking fast and loud on the sidewalk, she tried to imagine who could have done it, or what might have happened. As she pondered the mystery and the wonder of what seemed like being born again, she noticed something else: Although Columbus Street was level, the way home seemed downhill.

To fully understand the beauty of sunlight, you must spend some time in the dark. To fully understand — and appreciate — the gifts of hope and forgiveness that Jesus shares with us, we must understand how truly desperate and hopeless our situations are without them. We each owe a debt that we can't possibly pay, ourselves — but if we will just open our hearts to him, offer ourselves to him, believe in the gift that he offers, Jesus will be there to pay it off for us.

Lent 4
John 9:1-41
by Peter Andrew Smith

The Disturbing Witness of Grace

"Why?" Susan asked.

Everyone tensed around the table and no one met her gaze. People shifted uncomfortably in their seats as her question echoed in the room.

"We are not going to reconsider our decision," the chairperson said as he adjusted his glasses.

"I'm aware of that," Susan said. "I simply want to know why you do not want to hire me, since I have the degree, experience, and am willing to accept what you are able to pay."

"You are not a suitable person to be our youth minister," the chairperson said. "Our decision is final."

"Yes," she said trying to keep her voice calm. "I understand that. I even grudgingly accept that. But what I do not understand is why you think I am unacceptable to teach young people."

"We don't have to give an explanation," he repeated.

"Since you called me to come to this second interview I think you owe me an explanation," she said.

The shifting of the committee members in their chairs increased and they continued to look away from her.

"We discovered after you were invited to this meeting that you do not have suitable character," the chairperson said. "Let us leave it at that."

"That isn't good enough. My references are impeccable, my previous work experience is...."

The chairperson slammed his pen onto the desk. "You

made those movies. There is no way that we are going to let someone who did such degenerate things teach about Jesus and his love to our young people."

Susan looked down. "I did some things that I am not proud of when I was younger." She looked up. "That was before I came to know Jesus in my life."

"That doesn't matter," he said. "A youth minister is supposed to be a role model, the children are going to look up to you. You have to have impeccable character."

Everyone around the room murmured in agreement.

"I agree completely," Susan said. "Any minister of the church should live the message of Jesus in their life. I did not know about God's love for me when I did those things. I thank God that one night I wandered into a church during a service and heard the preacher tell about forgiveness and grace. I cried that whole night when I realized that I didn't have to live the way I was living. I changed that day. By God's love and through God's grace I left the life I had been in and I have never looked back."

She took a deep breath. "Eventually I realized that God was calling me to work with young people as a minister and I studied, worked, and served the church in that way. As you can see I have been in a number of churches setting up successful youth programs and Sunday schools —"

"None of that matters," the chairperson said waving his hands. "We are not hiring you. You do not have suitable character to work with children. If they ever learned that you had made those movies...."

"Or actually saw clips from one of them," one of the women piped in.

"Exactly!" the chairperson said. "We would lose all credibility as a church."

"I don't advertise my past indiscretions. But in the internet age no sin like mine stays hidden long." Susan looked the chairperson in the eyes. "It came up at the last church I worked at as a youth minister. Some teenage girls asked me. I was honest about what I did and told the teens the truth about how it demeans and diminishes what God intends for us and our bodies. I was firm that the path I was on at their age is filled with lies, hurt, and harm both physical and spiritual. I also told them that I know God can forgive anything and everything through Jesus and offers us a fresh chance to live differently."

"And is that why you are looking for a new church? Because people found out?"

Susan shook her head. "I spoke to the church board the day after I spoke to the teens. With the blessing of the church board, I worked another five years at that church. I'm here because my husband took a transfer to this city."

The chairperson scowled. "I cannot comment about the irresponsible actions of the churches you were at before. But hearing your story means nothing to me. All I know is that we have no place for a sinner like you among us."

A murmur of agreement echoed in the room from the other committee members.

"I'm sorry that my story doesn't make a difference to you," Susan said as she picked up her papers to leave. "I'll pray that one day it will matter to you because I don't know how you can be a church without knowing grace and the one who gives it."

Lent 5
Ezekiel 37:1-14
by John Smylie

Bones

Growing up in the suburbs, I didn't have a lot of opportunity to come across bones. Yes of course there were bones for dogs, steak bones, and milk bones, but I didn't run into a lot of bones in the manicured yards of friends and neighbors. Occasionally I would run into a dead mouse brought home to be admired by one of our Siamese cats but then one really only saw a limp and fleshy body of those poor creatures.

In the summers, we would head for the wilderness. As a family, we would pack up the station wagon with the rear seat facing out the back window. Dad would have one of the boats that he made during the winter trailing behind and we would drive for over eight hours through the Appalachian Mountains on the way to New Hampshire. We were very blessed to be able to rent a cottage on a beautiful and primitive lake. The cottage, also called a camp, was very rustic. The main room surrounded the large fireplace and at one end there was a staircase that led up to the second floor on which there was a balcony that surrounded the entire living room. There were several bedrooms and bathrooms off the balcony. At the far ends of the second floor and visible from the living room there were two large heads. One was of a moose the other appeared to be a very large buck. On the second floor across from the fireplace there was a skull. I never was quite sure what it was and I think that was my first experience of old dry bones. It's probably a good thing that the Lord didn't come into that space and stir up those old bones, certainly I would have been terrified as a child to see that moose or that deer or that skull come off the wall and come alive.

Several years ago, my wife had an encounter with bones. It was an autumn day and I was in my home office working on a church project when from the garage I heard her scream, calling me to come. I don't remember ever having heard her sound so shaken up before. I had no idea what it was that she could be screaming about. I left my office immediately and found her trembling in the garage pointing to a little skull on the floor next to our five-month-old puppy. He had brought home what he thought was a treasure from the woods.

Earlier that year Jill's faithful golden retriever of many years had to be put down. He was suffering greatly and could no longer even get up on his legs. We have a veterinarian who lives across the street from us in our home in Spokane who came over and took a look at Buddy. After a few moments, he recommended to us that we take him and have him put to sleep. He couldn't do it for us at our own home; we had to go to a local veterinarian who performed the task. The veterinarian asked if we would like to be with him when he died I said yes as did our youngest child; Jill declined. We went in and had Buddy put to sleep. He had been such a fine animal — polite, respectful, and he would never enter the house without first being invited. It felt right to assist him in his last journey and though it was difficult, we both were glad to be in the room with him when he breathed his last breath.

In the springtime of that year, I decided that I would surprise Jill with a new puppy. I looked through the paper over the course of a couple weeks until it appeared that there would be a good selection of puppies for us to look at. Though there's no way of replacing one living creature with another, we knew that we liked golden retrievers and there was a new litter of golden retrievers with eight puppies available to pick out and pick up. We drove from Spokane into northern

Idaho and found a humble home with a tired-looking mother golden retriever caring for eight lively little creatures. After spending time with each one of the puppies, we decided on a particular male that seemed to have a subdued personality. There was something quite aristocratic about his nature and we thought he would be a bit easier to raise than some of the other more rambunctious little personalities that were running around on four legs.

We brought him home and named him Reilly. I don't know why we named him that it just felt right at the time. He was an excellent puppy. I will always remember the first time I put him on a leash and we walked down to the mailbox, which is a mile away from our home. Never once did he tug on the leash, the entire time he was on my right keeping in perfect step. I couldn't believe how well mannered and how adult he was behaving. Reilly enjoyed sleeping in the garage. One evening he disappeared. We wondered if perhaps someone had taken him. We also knew that there were coyotes in the area and we wondered if the coyotes had gotten hold of him during the night. I kept hoping he would return, but hours turned into days, and days turned into weeks, and we knew that Reilly would not be returning.

At the end of summer, I took one of our children and went off on an evening adventure and found another little golden retriever puppy that I brought home. We named him RJ, which stands for Reilly Jr. He was a lot different than the original Reilly; in fact he still is. He is anything but aristocratic. The first time he went on a leash he pulled me the entire time. He's a sweetheart of an animal but far less disciplined than his namesake though over time he has grown to be better behaved. Our house in Spokane has a good deal of wooded area all around it. As RJ grew older, he enjoyed exploring the woods. On this particular day, the day that I heard Jill screaming in the garage, RJ had brought home a skull. Looking at the skull, I knew immediately that he had solved the mystery of Reilly's death. It was Reilly's skull that RJ brought back to our garage. That sweet life was now represented by a dry bone.

As sad as it was to discover that Reilly had died such a cruel death most likely by coyotes, it was also good to know what had happened to him. We now knew better how to pray for him, even at the time of his death, praying that his suffering was minimal, hoping that he would know our care for him even as he faced the horrors that sometimes occur in the natural world. I'm not sure bones are ever pleasant to come across because they represent a life that is no longer with us. I am sure that our Lord breathes life into our bones. Some of us may feel we have old bones that could use a little of the Spirit's breath upon us. Ezekiel lets us know that even the old dry bones, lost bones, and forgotten bones, the bones covered by sand and bleached by the sun, these old bones can have new life breathed into them.

Perhaps today as we reflect upon the good news that we find in the Spirit breathing life into the old bones that lay in the tomb, or bones that are scattered in the woods or bleached white under the desert sun, perhaps we can find hope in the deaths we have faced in our lifetime, knowing and believing that our Lord is able to reconstruct, bring alive, renew, refresh, and even cause old bones to be reborn. I think in God's time I'll get to see Buddy again, and Reilly who lived for such a short time, and my dad who lived a faithful life, and my grandfather who used to play with me when I was a little boy and my first wife who was a soul mate. All these who have gone before, who now are little more than bone and ash, I believe can and will have the Spirit blow upon them and on the last day they will arise and join in the triumphal procession through the pearly gates and walk upon the golden streets of heaven.

Passion / Palm Sunday
Matthew 26:14—27:66
by David O. Bales

Is It Truth?

Near the city of Rome in the year later numbered 49 AD, Aaron's father brought Aaron, then ten years old, to a synagogue where they'd never been. Only male believers in Jesus were summoned. They received two days' notice: "Every male member of a household believing in Christ must arrive at the synagogue in the port city of Ostia by midday."

As soon as Aaron and his father entered the synagogue, his father pointed Aaron to the other boys and told him to wait with them. His father joined the thirty or so men speaking softly as they huddled in a corner. Aaron was pleased to see Caleb among the other boys. Caleb was two years older than Aaron and he made it his business to answer all of Aaron's questions. "What's going on?" Aaron asked. "Abba just said we had to come but he didn't say why."

"Something about the emperor," Caleb said. He looked around quickly. "When we left home early this morning Imma was crying."

"My Imma hugged me so hard it hurt," Aaron said.

Caleb began to say, "Abba thinks they might want us out of the city so they can..." when the synagogue's front door opened. Four fully equipped soldiers entered, leading an old man. For a few heartbeats no Jew moved or spoke. One soldier stepped forward and announced in Latin and then repeated himself in Greek, "Over here. Listen to this man." The Jewish males turned toward the soldiers and the old man with them. The old man was dressed as a Jew. Aaron scurried to his father's side, glancing at the soldiers' swords as he did.

The soldiers stepped back and blocked the door. A few men turned to look at the other door. Soldiers had stepped in quietly from the back also. The adults all looked around desperately. The old man raised his hand and spoke, "Peace. Peace," he said in Aramaic. "It is well. It is well."

Aaron could tell that his father's hearing the man speak in Aramaic helped him relax a little.

"I've been sent by Emperor Claudius, savior of the world, benefactor of humankind, patron of art and reverence. May he prosper and may sacrifices in Jerusalem continue to be offered for his well-being."

The Jewish men shuffled their feet or looked down at this description of the emperor, but all remained silent.

"I've come to remind us Jews how reverently and benevolently the empire has treated us. We are exempted from military service, are we not? Our obedience to the holy sabbath is honored, is it not? And even though many of us dwell in Rome because Pompey brought our great-grandfathers here as slaves, we witness to how quickly our people here have been granted freedom."

The old man paused and stroked his beard. "Now, however, some of you have provoked other Jews to riot because of this Jesus. So the government that protects all lands and seas informs you now for your own good about the Jesus you call Messiah. The truth that our faithful auxiliary legions reported nearly a generation ago is that a man named Jesus Barabbas was crucified in Jerusalem by Pilate — not Jesus of Nazareth. Barabbas was a great hero of our people. He offered himself in place of the Nazarene, who was a simple country teacher who in Jerusalem found himself confused when opposition mounted and his supporters abandoned him."

Aaron looked up at his father who held his lips tightly shut and his eyes straight forward.

"An unfortunate misunderstanding arose that Jesus of Nazareth was killed and was magically restored to the living.

This mistaken report has been twisted twenty different ways by 100 fools around the sea in the middle of the inhabited world. The certified report states that Jesus died a few years later in Bethlehem and some of his sincere and grief-stricken students snatched his body from his family and buried him not in a tomb, but in a grave in the Essene cemetery by the Dead Sea. His grave remains there beside that of his Uncle Zechariah for anyone to inspect."

Aaron's thoughts were pounding through his ten-year-old head. He had learned that Jesus suffered and that God resurrected him, proving he was the Messiah. Aaron nudged his father's hand to ask a question, but his father shushed him.

The old man began to speak slower, pausing between each word, "Remember, I tell you this as the Emperor's messenger... with your safety in the balance."

Without another word or gesture, he turned and the soldiers with him followed as he exited. The soldiers who had been at the rear door, instead of leaving as they came, paraded through the synagogue to leave by the front door.

To Aaron the gasps and sighs that followed sounded as though everyone started to breathe again. He grabbed his Father's hand firmly this time and tugged him down. "Abba, is it truth?"

A man was speaking to his father on his other side and everyone was moving quickly toward the synagogue's door. His father pulled Aaron hastily from the building as he said, "Son, if Jesus hasn't been raised from the dead, you can say that anything is true. Now hang on to Abba's hand."

Aaron held tightly as other grandfathers, fathers, and sons scurried toward home. He and Caleb saw one another as their fathers yanked them into different groups scurrying back toward Rome. Before they lost sight of each other, Aaron and Caleb gave one another a confused wave.

Maundy Thursday
1 Corinthians 11:23-26
by C. David McKirachan

Do This Remembering Me...

Sometimes I wonder how we've gotten to the stilted ceremonial enactment of the fellowship meal that was the beginning and the core of the Christian experience. We use starched linens and little shot glasses loaded into silver trays like bullets into a magazine. Then there's the cubed wonder bread. I worry sometimes that in our effort to be faithful to the Lord, we forget him by making this gift of sharing he gave us into a dry ritual.

What are we supposed to remember? We're supposed to remember him. We're supposed to remember his life — his vibrant, real, messy life. We're supposed to remember his passion to share the glory of God's presence in every moment, in spite of the obtuseness of his friends and followers. We're supposed to remember his insistence on pushing his disciples closer to each other and closer to God, in spite of their desires to be individuals and run their own agendas and maintain control. We're supposed to remember his compassion and empathy that realized and understood all the hang-ups and fears and foibles of these people who sat around him, and his forgiveness and deep, deep hope for their growth beyond all the idiocies. We're supposed to remember his joy at the smallest and most glorious bits and pieces of life. We're supposed to remember his sorrow and grief at the shadows that they preferred to the light of all that glory. And we're supposed to remember his love that infused each and every word he said and movement he made.

Does all of that come through our ritual? Does he stand in our midst?

No. And yes.

The mystery of our feast is not in our excellence but in his presence. We're no better than they were. We're obtuse and confused and hung up and angry and judgmental and controlling and afraid and self-centered and hard-hearted, just like they were — and he still comes among us. Once in a while, as the bread is broken, his hand scarred by our sin, rests on our shoulder and calls us beloved.

And we remember him.

Good Friday
Isaiah 52:13—53:12
by Frank Ramirez

Reflecting Martyrs

> *Surely he has borne our infirmities and carried our diseases; yet we accounted him stricken, struck down by God, and afflicted. He was wounded for our transgressions, crushed for our iniquities; upon him was the punishment that made us whole, and by his bruises we are healed.*
> — Isaiah 53:4-5

In the eyes of some people, the Amish are the stuff of postcards, quaint men with long beards and women in black bonnets riding horse and buggy as a vague rejection of modernism. It is often forgotten by tourists that their lifestyle is based on their fierce commitment to live every aspect of their lives as disciples of Jesus. "What would Jesus do?" is not a slogan for a bracelet but a question that is not only asked but also answered and then lived.

If any were ignorant of this fact they were simply not paying attention after the killing of five Amish girls at the Nickel Mines schoolhouse on October 2, 2006, referred to by the Amish as their own 9/11.

One of the most striking aspects of the Nickel Mines murders was the way the families of the victims and the Amish at large immediately visited the family of the murderer and extended forgiveness and grace. They also shared a portion of the financial contributions that came streaming in from around the world with the killer's family.

Also memorable was the way one of the older girls in the one-room schoolhouse told the murderer to shoot her first. Her intent was to allow others to live by dying first.

To the Amish this self-sacrifice, this willingness to die for others, comes as naturally as the ability to forgive. For them this is what it means to take the Sermon on the Mount seriously. If scripture were not enough, Amish children grow up with stories from the immense volume known as *The Martyr's Mirror*, stories that make such actions automatic.

The Martyr's Mirror, published in 1660, tells the story of those Christians, including Mennonites and other Anabaptists, who died at the hands of other Christians because they chose to serve Jesus rather than acknowledge the lordship of Caesar. The book connects the suffering of faithful Christians who chose to be baptized as adults rather than be part of the state churches of Europe, with the faithfulness of martyrs in all ages. You will find a copy of this book in nearly all Amish homes.

One of the most famous stories, well known to Amish children and told as an example of the selfless love that all Christians should have, is that of Dirk Willems. In the year 1569, Dirk was arrested by the religious authorities in Asperen, Holland, for having held Bible studies in his home and for having been baptized as an adult. The account of his arrest follows:

> Concerning his apprehension, it is stated by trustworthy persons, that when he fled he was hotly pursued by a thiefcatcher, and as there had been some frost, said Dirk Willems ran before over the ice, getting across with considerable peril. The thiefcatcher following him broke through, when Dirk Willems, perceiving that the former was in danger of his life, quickly returned and aided him in getting out, and thus saved his life. The thiefcatcher wanted to let him go, but the burgomaster, very sternly called to him to consider his oath, and thus he was again seized by the thiefcatcher, and, at said place, after severe imprisonment and great trials ... put to death at a lingering fire by these bloodthirsty, ravening wolves, enduring it with great steadfastness,

> and confirming the genuine faith of the truth with his death and blood, as an instructive example to all pious Christians of this time.

Having saved his rescuer, Dirk Willems endured a particularly gruesome death. *The Martyr's Mirror* notes:

> In this connection, it is related as true from the trustworthy memoirs of those who were present at the death of this pious witness of Jesus Christ, that the place where this offering occurred was without Asperen, on the side of Leerdam, and that, a strong east wind blowing that day, the kindled fire was much driven away from the upper part of his body, as he stood at the stake; in consequence of which this good man suffered a lingering death, insomuch that in the town of Leerdam, toward which the wind was blowing, he was heard to exclaim over seventy times: "O my Lord; my God," etc., for which cause the judge or bailiff, who was present on horseback, filled with sorrow and regret at the man's sufferings, wheeled about his horse, turning his back toward the place of execution, and said to the executioner: "Dispatch the man with a quick death." But how or in what manner the executioner then dealt with this pious witness of Jesus, I have not been able to learn, except only, that his life was consumed by the fire, and that he passed through the conflict with great steadfastness, having commended his soul into the hands of God.

For Amish children, Dirk Willems and other men and women like him are as real as George Washington and Abraham Lincoln are to what they refer to as "the English," their term for non-Amish. The stories of *The Martyr's Mirror* bring to life those who have practiced nonresistance to evil and self-sacrifice even to the point of death for others. The example of Jesus is not just theoretical — Amish children know that his example on Calvary's hill has been emulated by thousands and thousands.

As we begin to contemplate the sacrifice of Jesus let us also think about what stories in our lives, if any, ever really challenge us to truly follow in his footsteps.

Source: Donald B. Kraybill, Steven M. Nolt, and David L. Weaver-Zercher, *Amish Grace: How Forgiveness Transcended Tragedy* (San Francisco: John Wiley & Sons, 2007)

You can download *The Martyr's Mirror* at www.martyrsmirror.com.

Easter Sunday
Acts 10:34-43; Colossians 3:1-4
by Argile Smith

Anticipation

Coach Clark had led the men's basketball team to one of the biggest winning streaks in the high school's recent memory, even though the beginning of the season had been tough. That's when two of the starters had to be sidelined. Without them, the season looked bleak. The new players who had moved into their places seemed to have some problems adjusting to the others on the team. They couldn't make themselves fit well into the team's routine or rhythm. Over and over, Coach Clark tried to fix the problem caused by the new players, but nothing worked. Consequently, he feared that the team would be doomed to one tragic loss after another and that the remainder of the season would be characterized by gut-wrenching misery for everyone involved.

Not long into the season, however, things began to click for the team. Much to Coach Clark's surprise, the team started to work together and hit a rhythm that produced points on the scoreboard. By the end of the season, the team had gained momentum with a winning spree and had almost made it all the way to the championship game. Although they didn't get as far as the championship, the guys on the team felt good about what would happen next season.

The anticipation continued to grow after the season ended. Conversations among students, teachers, parents, and other people in the community revolved around what would happen next year. The more they talked about it, the more they speculated about how many games they would win. Their speculations fueled their excitement over the possibility of a winning season and a shot at the championship.

When Coach Clark gathered the team for training just before the new season commenced, he knew that everyone was still talking about what lay ahead. The hope of a winning season filled the air, and he knew it.

After he gave the players a chance to warm up on the court, he blew his whistle and called for everyone to take a seat on the bleachers near him. They reacted like winning players, eagerly finding their seats and situating themselves to listen to what their coach had to say to them.

Coach Clark started by thanking each of the players for staying with the team another year. He went on to affirm their talents, their fine finish last season, and the sense of anticipation regarding the future of the team. Then he elaborated on the tough beginning they endured and the happy ending they enjoyed together.

"Men," he explained, "the team came back to life after everyone had given us up for dead. When we started to come alive, people began to believe in us again. Now they're sure that we have a winning season on our hands."

After a long pause, he asserted, "But men, we're not back in last season when things started to turn around for us. And we're not playing the championship game yet either. Right now we're in the middle, somewhere between having the breath put back in our lungs last season and winning the championship next season. If what happened in the past means anything to us and if we anticipate something good happening in the future, we've got to make the most of the time in the middle."

That's when he instructed them to practice the plays more, work the court better, and shoot the ball with more accuracy. After talking about what he wanted to accomplish during pre-season training, he said, "Remember that we've experienced a resurrection of sorts. We believe that the season ahead of us looks promising. Now keep on telling yourself that you have an opportunity right now to make the most of what's here in the middle."

The resurrection of Christ breathed new life into his followers, and we anticipate a promising future because of it. The anticipation of Easter helps us as we live productively for him right now, somewhere in the middle.

Easter 2
John 20:19-31
by Keith Hewitt

Tracks

It had snowed again — a late season dusting, a thin layer of fresh powder like a clean, white sheet thrown over the bones of Old Man Winter. They stepped out onto the stoop, and as the man pulled the door shut his son leaned over and studied two lines of markings in the snow. "What's that?" he asked, pointing at the tracks in the pristine white snow.

His father glanced at his watch, then looked down at the tracks. Each line was like a series of dots, almost one in front of the other. Looking closer, the dots resolved into four-toed paw prints; looking closer still, the procession of prints actually formed a kind of double line, with the paw prints marching silently on either side of an imaginary line. "Those are cat tracks," he said, and pointed with a gloved finger. "See how each one is almost in front of the one behind it, alternating to one side or the other? That's how cats walk."

"Must be a big cat," his son judged. "The paws are almost a foot apart." He pointed back, to where the tracks came around the corner of the house and then cut through the yard, across the stoop, down the sidewalk, and onto the driveway — perfectly parallel and rail-straight.

"I don't think so," the father answered, "Come on." They walked to the driveway, the boy taking care not to step on the tracks. They got to the driveway, and he said, "See, there."

The left line of prints peeled off suddenly, going down the driveway between the clear spot where his wife's van and his daughter's car had been parked. The other line went around the front of his daughter's car, then cut down between her car and his. "It's two cats!" the boy said excitedly, and ran the couple of steps to where the tracks split. "See! This one went down there, and this one went over by your car!" As he talked, the words came out in puffs of clouds, warm breath expelled into cold air.

"Looks that way," his father agreed.

"Were they chasing one another?"

"I don't think so — the stride doesn't seem to be very long." He glanced at his watch again, then in spite of himself looked around the driveway. "Here," he said, after a moment. He walked down the driveway to where the van had been parked, stepping in the clear space, stopping at the end nearest the street. His son hurried over to where he stood, looked down at the tracks in the snow, where he pointed.

"A rabbit?" the boy wondered, gauging the short stretch of tracks coming from under a bush — this was a pattern of two long prints, side by side, with a pair of smaller prints between them and toward the back, almost one in front of the other. If he closed his eyes, he could almost see it hop out from under the bush, cross the bit of driveway to the van, and then disappear under it.

But where to, then? He looked around, walked to the other end of the clear spot, now slowly starting to get covered with an airbrushing of white, fluffy snow as the wind picked up. There! "He went under the van here, then came out from under by the tire at the other end — back toward the garage."

"Yep," his father agreed. "Maybe trying to dodge the cats." He nodded toward the car, then. "Let's go, or we'll be late."

Reluctantly, his son walked back to the car, eyes scanning as his head swiveled from side to side, trying to spot the animals. As he crossed in front of his father's car, he stopped, stared at the hood for a moment, then laughed and pointed. "Looks like someone else was here too!"

His father paused from opening the door, looked at the hood. A line of paw prints started in the middle, appearing out of nowhere, then proceeded down to the front left corner, back across the hood, up to the windshield, and off. These were a series of "V" shapes, two four-toed prints in the back, two larger five-toes prints in the front.

"Was it another cat?" his son wondered.

"I don't think so. They're too small, and not the right shape." He looked around, then looked up — and nodded. "Those are squirrel tracks. See, it came out on that branch, there —" he pointed to a thick, leafless branch hanging over his car, "— jumped down on the car, then ran around and jumped off."

"Cool! Maybe he was avoiding the cats too."

"Maybe. Now let's get going, or we'll be late for church."

All the way there, the boy talked about the tracks they had found, even as the wind peeled the evidence off the car's hood and dusted over that which was left behind at home. His mother was just finishing her meeting as they arrived, and he ran up to hug her. "Mom!" he said excitedly, "we had all kinds of animals running around our house this morning!"

"Really? I didn't see any animals when I left for church."

"Neither did we," he said, "but we know they were there — we saw the tracks!"

"Then it's just like God," she said.

"What do you mean?" he asked.

"I mean you never really see him — but you can look at what he's done in the world around you, and know he's been there."

The reality of our faith is that only a handful of followers ever saw the risen Savior. We can cluck our tongues at Thomas, and chide him for doubting because he hadn't seen

— but in the end, we are not that different. We have not seen the wounds, put our hands in the holes, but we do not believe without proof, either.

It's just a different kind of proof — a faith-driven proof.

We see the proof of God's love in the world around us. Every act of mercy, every kindness of one human to another, every moment of grace comes about because God touches the human heart, and the heart acts. We feel the power of God's love inside us, the energy and peace that should not go together, but somehow do, as they fill the void in our souls left by sin.

We do not need to touch Jesus' wounds, because we can touch our own, and wonder at the healing that God has wrought in us... and know that Jesus is among us still.

Easter 3
Acts 2:14a, 22-32
by John Smylie

Speak the Truth in Love

Peter, standing with the eleven, raised his voice and addressed them: "Therefore let the entire house of Israel know with certainty that God has made him both Lord and Messiah, this Jesus whom you crucified."

It seems to me there is a temptation among Christians to be nice. Peter, in addressing this crowd is anything but nice. He loves, but he is not nice.

It takes a lot of confidence to be able to speak the truth without the fear of repercussions. Peter has come to that place having experienced the depth of his own weakness. It wasn't that long ago that he denied his Lord three times when his Lord was in his most vulnerable moments. Peter has obviously done a whole lot of growing since then and now he himself was willing to put himself at risk to speak the truth.

I have a friend who has a gift of being able to speak the truth in love, in pastoral situations, from the pulpit and in almost every walk of life. Somehow those, at least most of those who hear him, love the fact that he is willing to challenge them. I think they love him because they know that he cares for them and is willing to risk his own relationship with them because he loves them so much. He is the best pastor I have ever met. I have known him to confront the powerful and the meek. I have known him to confront bishops, fellow clergy, government officials, and others.

There was one time when he was at a funeral of a friend who was being buried from a Roman Catholic church. My friend is an Episcopal clergyman and he was dressed in his clerical collar while attending a service. He had no role in conducting the service. He simply was one of those who sits in the pew to worship the Lord, pray for the family, and care for those in attendance while honoring the departed. When it was time to receive communion only the Roman Catholics in attendance at the service were invited to receive the sacrament. Apparently, these are the rules. Something inside my friend got stirred up and he felt called to come forward and receive the sacrament. For him the sacrament meant being connected not only with Christ but with the gathered community and with the departed. For him to skip the sacramental meal that was being offered would have been an insult to the family of his friend and to his friend whose life they had gathered to celebrate. So he disregarded the instruction of the priest — that this was for Roman Catholics only — and he came forward and knelt at the altar rail with hands stretched out to receive the Body of Christ.

When the Roman Catholic priest came by he refused to give the sacrament to my friend. My friend then said to him, "You have to give it to me." The priest again refused. My friend then said to him, "If this is the Body of Christ, you have to give it to me." My friend wasn't going anywhere. The Catholic priest was becoming angry. My friend then asked him, "Is this just some Roman Catholic thing or is it the Body of Christ? If it's the Body of Christ you must give it to me." The Catholic priest then placed the sacrament in my friend's hand saying to him, "You will see me in my office after the service." I don't know what happened in the office but I do know that my friend spoke the truth with love to the Roman priest and perhaps even to the Catholic church. It didn't matter to him if it was a local priest, the bishop, or even the Pope administering the sacrament. What mattered to him was the connection that was found in the bread and in the wine — a connection to the living God — a connection to the community gathered — a connection to the God of the living — a connection to his departed friend.

Some of us come by this talent naturally — the talent of speaking the truth in love — others of us, like Peter, may learn this the hard way. Early on in my ministry, I was more concerned with being liked than I was with speaking the truth. I hadn't named that within myself at that time but later I came to learn that this was true — one of my weaknesses — one of my flaws. When we discover we are among those who were more interested in being liked and pleasing others than we are in speaking the truth in love, we may discover that we have an opportunity to grow. Being nice and seeking to please others rather than speaking the truth in love leads to a very empty and hollow feeling and certainly does nothing to advance Christianity.

As we learn this lesson — as we risk speaking the truth in love — we become more substantive — more whole — more like Christ. I recently had an opportunity to speak the truth in love to an older gentleman who was making life-and-death decisions.

Roger was in and out of the hospital. Over the last several months it seemed that he was spending more and longer stays there. The quality of his life was deteriorating and he was afraid that he was becoming a burden to all those around him, especially his wife, Doris. His heart was failing. The medications that he was taking were becoming more difficult to manage. The internal defibrillator had become a burden that he no longer wanted to bear. His life was slowly ebbing away and he was growing more frustrated with the experience.

After much reflection, discussion with family, his doctors, and his priest, Roger decided that he was ready to stop treatment. To continue on would be to continue on the same path — the same downward spiral — more time in the hospital, less time at home — and he was unwilling to stay on that path. He made the decision to turn off the internal defibrillator and to wean himself away from the medications. He now would qualify for hospice care. He lived in a community that had a residential hospice unit — a home that he could move into and spend his last days under hospice care. His family could visit as often as they liked — unlimited visiting hours. In his mind, he wanted to make the transition from this life to the next as easy for his wife Doris as he could. He did not want to burden her even though hospice would offer on-site care for him if he chose to go to his home.

Doris was very clear that she wanted Roger to come home and die in the place that he loved, surrounded by family and the normalcy of everyday life. She wanted to be near him and have him hear the sounds of grandchildren in the house, breathe the aroma of wonderful meals being prepared in the kitchen, and experience the normalcy of the ordinary where God may be found most often. Roger didn't want to hear anything of this; he was determined to make life easier for Doris, and he was convinced he knew better. This is where I was invited to enter the conversation. This is where I felt I was called to speak the truth in love to my friend Roger. I had already affirmed his decision to put himself in God's care and allow himself to retreat from the extraordinary medical care that he was receiving. We had spent time reflecting on death as a part of life. What I needed to do here was to challenge Roger to receive the kindness, compassion, dedication, and love of his wife. He was being stubborn and, of course, the temptation was to pity him because of his situation. I did not pity him; in fact I believe with God's grace I was able to speak to him truth in love. When I challenged Roger to stop being so stubborn and listen to his wife and receive her deep and abiding love for him and go home and die there, he looked at me and smiled.

Roger received the word of his priest. Roger received the grace and kindness and compassion and love of his wife.

Roger has been received into the gracious and loving arms of his Lord.

Peter spoke the truth with love to those who had rejected Jesus. He told them of their mistake, perhaps knowing full well that he himself might be a victim of the same cruelty his Lord experienced — the same rejection — even a similar death. Peter was willing to give these folks a chance to do the right thing — a chance to turn around, a chance to repent, a chance to experience the good news of the risen Lord for themselves.

Speaking the truth in love really is all about caring for another. Our Lord's entire life is a witness to speaking the truth in love, and each of us is invited to join in his great mission with all that we say, with all that we do, with all that we have, and with all that we are.

Easter 4
Psalm 23
by C. David McKirachan

Familiar Words

The 23rd Psalm is good stuff. It says deep and meaningful things about God and about us. It confronts, comforts, and assures. Yup. But there is something more about this one. It sings in a voice that resonates deeper than any meaningful words could reach. There is something about the cadence and the touch of "The Lord is my shepherd..." that reminds us of who we are in a way that other, just as profound words do not.

She was in the nursing home when I moved here, more than a decade ago. She had been "out of it" for years before that. She didn't know anyone and sat and stared into some distance beyond the horizons I could see. Then she lost what consciousness she had and slipped into a coma. I went to see her once in a while. I'd sit and talk to her. Tell her things that were going on with her friends and in the church.

One evening I got a call that she wasn't "long for this world." As I drove over, I wondered where she'd been all these years, between here and there. I wondered if she had to come back to leave. I wondered...

The nurse told me she'd been peaceful, but her breathing had changed and her vitals were dropping. I leaned over and smoothed back her hair, as I'd done before and came close to her ear. I whispered, "Wherever you've been, or wherever you're going, you're going with God." And I started whispering "The Lord is my shepherd..." She straightened in bed and opened her eyes, not wide, but wide enough to see me. And she started softly saying the psalm with me. She was hoarse, it had been a long time since she used that voice, but she stuck to it.

When we got to "...forever," she closed her mouth and smiled, a soft and satisfied smile and then closed her eyes and settled in. I heard the nurse move and looked up. She almost stuttered, "She hasn't spoken in years." "Well, maybe she finally had something important to say."

I don't know what circuit the psalm closed. I don't care if it reminded her of her childhood or her hope. I do know that something in those words and that rhythm called to her through all the fog and cobwebs and let her connect. She died an hour later, slipping off into an untroubled sleep.

It's good stuff, that psalm. Better than we know.

Easter 5
John 14:1-14
by Scott Dalgarno

Please Don't Forget Me

When we visit my wife's father, Henry (Hank, as everybody knows him), it's my job to prepare the scrambled eggs. On the particular morning I'm remembering, the day after Thanksgiving, I crack the eggs while my daughter Sarah cuts fruit into bowls — no grapefruit for her mother, lots of melon for her brother, and extra banana for her grandfather. I try hard to make sure the eggs are not runny, but not dry either.

Soon everyone is seated at the family table made by Hank himself. There's a chair for everyone and one chair set aside for Hank's late wife, Edith, my children's most beloved grandmother. The cushion is covered with fabric from one of her cheery summer dresses.

"Who's the boy?" Hank asks, looking directly at our son. "That's your grandson, Stephen," my wife, Catherine says. Hank doesn't recognize any of us anymore, except, Catherine. Hank has had a series of strokes — the last one took most of his memory and has left his right side shriveled. The one thing his memory is clear on is Edith. She was the one thing in his life that really "worked." "Best decision I ever made," he used to say, and now he can't even remember what he did all his life, what a difference he made in the lives of so many young people at Syracuse University.

The family tradition was that Hank says grace at meals, which I used to find funny because until he was nearly sixty, he was a self-described agnostic. It was the realization, coming on the eve of old age, that he and Edith would not always be together (on this side of the grave) that made him begin to entertain the idea of heaven.

Maybe it was because she was such a beacon of goodness that he began to think the existence of such a place was even possible. Oh, there was nothing all that saintly about her. No, she had a wicked sense of humor — everyone knew that. But she was just so... so solid. Her integrity was absolute. She was the one person I've met in my life who really loved everybody. Some try, but Edith pulled it off, and there was no doubting it. I remember how suspect I was, meeting this amazing family the day that Catherine first brought me into her home. To Hank, I was Charles Manson until proven otherwise. But not for Edith. She read in the looks Catherine gave me at our first dinner around this same table that I was someone special, even if I didn't feel it myself, and until the day of her death she made me feel that I had given her the greatest two gifts in her life — her two grandchildren.

It was the day she died when something broke, for the first time, in Hank's steely composure. We all stood or sat around Grandma's bed and we were holding her hands, chatting quietly, and she just slipped away, as they say. No great labored breaths, no rattles, just a quiet letting go. We found ourselves transfixed by the smile that came to her mouth and eyes in that last moment. It wasn't lost on Hank. Whatever she was seeing, HE wanted to see. More than that, he wanted to go where she had told him she believed she was headed — the place she was sure she would see her own mother again, and the place she believed she would see the one who taught her it was possible to love people as if they were all children of God.

For Hank, heaven became a matter of trust, of trusting his wife. In those few moments beside her bed, his heart grew strangely warm. Where she was going, he wanted to go, and his sarcasm about spiritual matters evaporated right then and there.

Once the eggs and bowls of fruit were placed in front of

everyone we bowed our heads, grabbed hands, and waited. Hank didn't speak. After a few moments of silence Catherine began, "God is..." Hank chimed in, "God is..." That was followed by another long pause, at which point Stephen and Sarah started in slowly and deliberately. "God is good, God is great. Let us thank him for our food." Everyone added an "Amen" except Hank. He still had his head bowed. He seemed to be mumbling something. Catherine leaned over kissing his shoulder and rubbing his back very gently. Then she raised herself and settled her head on his shoulder looking about eighteen again. It nearly did me in.

After breakfast Catherine and I gathered up the dishes. I noticed tears in her eyes. "Are you all right?" I asked.

She hesitated and then said, "Dad was praying the same thing over and over. He just kept saying, 'God take care of Edith,' and 'God... please don't forget me. Please don't forget me. Please don't forget me....' "

Easter 6
Acts 17:22-31
by Peter Andrew Smith

Looking for God

There once was a man who wanted more in life. He believed there must be something greater than what he was experiencing, some grander purpose than just surviving day to day, some deeper meaning to connect to in his life, so he began to search.

He spent time considering the world around him and discovered that when he was outside in nature he felt connected to something greater than himself. Sitting on the seashore or watching the sunrise on a mountain, he felt something he did not feel in his everyday life. He wanted to experience and know that feeling all the time but could never control when it occurred.

The man tried to find what he sought by achieving perfect health. He exercised, ate healthy, and he stretched the limits of his body. As he engaged in physical activity, he discovered there were times when he felt alive like no other. Yet those occasions were fleeting and those times never lasted long.

The man who was searching tried to understand. He studied, researched, and learned. As he expanded his mind, he experienced occasions when he caught a glimpse of something more. At those times, he felt that he was close to what he was seeking, but those occasions also never lasted. No matter how much he studied and learned he could not truly understand what he sought.

The man used what he had seen in nature, what he had learned, and what he could do, to create. He fashioned things in words, paint, and clay. As the man created, he sometimes felt connected to what he sought. In the sentences, in the pictures from his imagination, as his hands sculpted, he felt more than himself but he was never able to completely capture what he desired in his art.

The man assumed he had failed in his search. He looked at what he had seen, felt, understood, and achieved and knew now more than ever that there was something missing in his life.

One day the man came upon another man and shared his story. He told of his searching, his desire to know the greater life, which always seemed just beyond him. The other man listened to the story of searching and told him of the God who had created all the earth, who fashioned humanity in the divine image, who knew everything and who was the source of inspiration and imagination. The man who had searched was excited as he heard of this God for he knew that the glimpses of something greater he had known in life must be of God.

When the other man told him that God had come to earth so that everyone could see, understand, and know God, the man began to weep. As he wept, he began to see the hand of God in the world around him, in the life he felt within him, in the understanding he had of the universe, and in the creativity he expressed. He dried his tears and realized he no longer had to search for God because God had found him.

Ascension of Our Lord
Acts 1:1-11
by Argile Smith

Wayne's Deployment

Wayne had his orders in his duffle bag when he walked through the door into Todd's room. A soldier who wanted to make a career out of military service, he knew that soon enough he would get an overseas assignment. That's why his deployment to Afghanistan didn't surprise him.

Being single made the assignment a little easier because he wouldn't leave behind a wife or children. Leaving his mom and dad and especially Todd, his little brother, turned out to be difficult enough. Going upstairs and walking through the door to Todd's bedroom to tell him good-bye tore at his heart.

He and Todd sat on the floor and talked about the assignment. Wayne reassured his little brother that he would return safe and sound. They talked about what they would do while they were separated and what they would do together once he came home. And then Wayne gave Todd that kind of hug known only to brothers who care about each other.

When the time had come for Wayne to leave, he said good-bye to his mom and dad who had been waiting downstairs. Todd walked with him down the steps. When Wayne hugged his parents, picked up his duffle bag, and walked outside to his car, Todd followed him. As Wayne drove away, Todd rushed to the street and watched as the taillights faded in the distance. For a long time he just stood there. Perhaps he hoped that Wayne would turn around and come home. Or maybe he regretted that he couldn't go with Wayne.

Soon his mom joined him in the street, and the two of

them stood together, weeping but saying nothing. His mom simply ran her hands through his hair like she had done so many times before when she sensed that he was upset about something. It was her way of consoling him without uttering a word. Actually, nothing could be said. Wayne had to go, and everyone who loved him had to stay.

But then she said, "Todd, Wayne's coming home. Just wait and see." And with that, the two of them walked back into the house, still weeping but now walking together in the resolve that they would be strong for each other and for Wayne.

Thanks to email messages, cell phone calls, and letters, Todd and his parents heard from Wayne more often than they anticipated. Wayne tried to keep them posted regularly on how things were going for him, the people he worked with, and — to a limited extent — the work he was doing.

A few months passed, and the family got some good news about Wayne. They found out that he had been given a promotion. Although the circumstances were sketchy, the point was clear. Wayne's superior officer recognized his potential for leadership and placed a significant number of soldiers under his command.

Not long afterward, Wayne's family found out about a commendation that he had received. Again, the information regarding the reason for the commendation was a little vague, but it had to do with meritorious service in the line of duty.

The details related to Wayne's promotion and commendation found a home in Todd's imagination. He investigated the kinds of metals and badges Wayne had been given, and he imagined them emblazoned on his brother's uniform. One day he would see Wayne coming home, bearing on his uniform all of the symbols of his success. Todd looked forward to his brother's return that much more.

The ascension of Jesus leaves with a similar batch of

mixed emotions. Separation, intimacy, and expectancy blend together in our hearts to strengthen our resolve to follow him.

Easter 7
John 17:1-11
by John Smylie

Where's the Finish Line?

I glorified you on earth by finishing the work that you gave me to do.
— John 17:4

For the last several weeks, there has been an enjoyable series of articles written by two women who are part of our local newspaper. One of them is a reporter who often gets her stories on the front page — she is young, attractive, and energetic. She has served in missionary activity and always appears to be up for a challenge. The other is also young and works more behind the scenes on the editorial staff of the paper. She is married, the mother of young children, and comes across in her reports as one who is quite humble and reflective.

The two of them have decided to run a marathon. That in itself is a very noble ambition. What makes this particular pact between them even more noble is the added obstacle of running the marathon in Colorado beginning in Estes Park where the elevation is way above one mile. In other words, the air is very thin and the training must take into account the lesser oxygen that is found at a higher elevation. The two of them are writing stories about their training as they prepare for the marathon this summer. Both of them come across as rather realistic and humble, admitting the times when they fall short in their training regimen. They reflect aloud about their own humanity. They invite the reader into their journey. Both of them wonder if they will finish the race. One of them, the mom, in a recent article has begun to lower her expectations. In chatting with her children, she's come to a kind of interior compromise that suggests that if she even begins the race and runs for more than a mile it will be sort of a personal victory.

The younger of the two also shares the kind of mind games that go on inside of her head as she prepares for this overwhelming task. At times, she chooses to leave her training regimen for the allure of an afternoon nap. I think why I'm so attracted to the two storytellers is that I find myself in the midst of both of their stories. It's so easy to set lofty goals. Perhaps for many of us our marathons are goals like losing 30 pounds that have crept on us over the last several years, or setting aside time to pray at least 45 minutes to an hour a day. Some of us seek to make it a priority to spend more time with our children and less time at work, yet we continue to fall short of this seemingly simple goal. Others determine that they will become more environmentally sensitive by driving their cars less and riding their bicycles and walking more. Some of us may seek to discipline ourselves to become less compulsive in our spending habits only to fall short when we see that irresistible pair of shoes that has our name written on them. On and on the list goes, the list that many of us renew at the end of each year with New Year's resolutions that are usually forgotten by January 15.

We won't know how the two newspaper women do until the summer but every one of us is challenged with similar goals perhaps not as lofty as a marathon but nevertheless challenges that call forth the best from us. Personally I hope the two ladies make it, I hope they're able not only to compete in the marathon but to finish the race even if it takes them several hours more than they anticipate, even if they have to walk across the finish line.

Many of us wonder what we have to do to make a difference in this world of ours. I think there may be something in human nature that is constantly calling us from the comfort of our lives into something more. I believe there is something noble, excellent, engaged, and even driven in the human spirit, something that lives within each of us; perhaps it could be described as a spark of the divine that calls us, moves us, and pushes us toward the divine and toward excellence. I believe that we are each made in the image of God. Though we may not yet understand how that gets to be lived out in the midst of us or through us, I believe there is something in us, a spirit and a life that longs to be lifted up and given to the world in a way that brings glory to God.

Often throughout the years of ministry, I have encountered wonderful and humble human beings who in reflective moments have questioned their value. These are human beings who have given much of themselves to making the world a brighter and better place who nevertheless wonder if their lives really make a difference. It seems to me that these questions arise in so many, particularly in the gifted — questions of value, questions of worth — and can only be answered by the divine. When Jesus said to his Father in heaven, "I glorified you on earth by finishing the work that you gave me to do," I believe he was referring not only to the work that he had done but to the work that he knew was in front of him.

Our Lord had begun his marathon when he was baptized in the Jordan River by his friend John. He continued his marathon when he went into the wilderness and fasted for forty days and forty nights and confronted the demons and temptations that, if not confronted, could cause him to fall short of his goal. He continued his race as he gathered disciples around him so he could teach them the way of salvation through being in relationship with them. Our Lord engaged in his marathon as he traveled throughout the length of the holy land preaching the good news, giving sight to the blind, hearing to the deaf, strengthening limbs to the lame, and even giving life to the dead. Our Lord ran his race as he challenged the religious and political systems of his day by pointing to a higher way, the way of his Father in heaven, the way of peace and humility and sacrifice. Even at the time of our Lord's praying this prayer that we hear in today's gospel text, our Lord begins to see the finish line and he knows that these last few miles will be the most difficult. He knows that these last few miles, where the air is thin and the pain is excruciating, are also the most important. For our Lord it wasn't so much about winning the race as it was about finishing the race. Finishing the race for him would demand that he not only be misunderstood, but also be willing to endure great suffering, the lashes of a whip, the piercing words and spit of the arrogant, the betrayal of his friends, the agonizing death and pain of crucifixion, and the hollowness of death.

In the midst of our questions, in the midst of our wondering where is the finish line for us, let us recognize that our Lord has already completed the race. Let us be open to the truth that our Lord is reaching out to us today, praying for us not only while he was here on earth but also from the heavens. Let us open ourselves today to the strength that he alone has given us and desires for us to receive. Our Lord did not accomplish his goal by merely relying on his willpower and his human strength. Our Lord accomplished his goal by connecting to his Father in heaven — by keeping focused on the prize that was to please his Father in heaven. His desire was not for himself but to bring glory to his Father in heaven and grace to us. Let us tap into the wellspring of life who can strengthen us to finish our race. Our Lord's endurance of the marathon that was set before him was aided by the strength given him from above. The same strength is available to us. May we also be willing to receive God's call and the desire to finish the race in a way that brings satisfaction to our souls and glory to our father in heaven and grace to those around us.

Lord, you are calling us to finish the race you have put

before us. Lord, you have called each of us to a unique and wonderful existence. Lord, you desire each of us to finish the race and we are well aware of our limitations. We are at times full of excuses and reasons why you have thought too highly of us. Lord, give us the grace to open ourselves to allow you to once again inspire and fill us with the divine spark, your presence, and your strength, so we may run toward the finish line you set in front of us knowing that you are lifting us, even carrying us when our legs are weak, our lungs are burning, and our minds are full of excuses. Let your heart beat within us, let your prayer carry us forward and may our lives surrender to you, giving you glory and grace to those around us.

About the Authors

David O. Bales was a Presbyterian (USA) pastor for 33 years, and is a graduate of the University of Portland (where he was editor of the yearbook) and San Francisco Theological Seminary. In addition to his ministry, he also has taught college: World Religions, Ethics, Biblical Hebrew and Biblical Greek (recently at College of Idaho). He has been a freelance researcher, writer, and editor for Stephen Ministries. His sermons and articles have appeared in *Interpretation*, *Pulpit Digest*, *Preaching*, *Lectionary Homiletics*, *Emphasis*, and *Preaching the Great Texts*. He wrote a year-long online column: "In The Original: Insights from Greek and Hebrew for the Lectionary Passages." His books include: *Gospel Subplots: Story Sermons of God's Grace*; *Toward Easter and Beyond*; *Scenes of Glory: Subplots of God's Long Story*; and *To the Cross and Beyond: Cycle A Sermons for Lent and Easter*, all available at CSS Publishing Company.

Scott Dalgarno is pastor of Wasatch Presbyterian Church in Salt Lake City, Utah. Born in California, he has previously served four Presbyterian churches in Oregon. He is a graduate of Whitworth University, University of Oregon, and San Francisco Theological Seminary. A poet, his poems have appeared in *The Christian Century*, *America*, *The Antioch Review*, and *Yale Review*.

Keith Hewitt is the author of three volumes of *NaTiVity Dramas: Nontraditional Christmas Plays for All Ages* (CSS). He is a local pastor, co-youth leader, an occasional speaker at Christmas events, and former Sunday school teacher at Wilmot United Methodist Church in Wilmot, Wisconsin. He lives in southeastern Wisconsin with his wife, two children, and assorted dogs and cats.

C. David McKirachan is pastor of the Presbyterian Church at Shrewsbury in central New Jersey. He also teaches at Monmouth University. McKirachan is the author of *I Happened Upon a Miracle* and *A Year of Wonder* (Westminster John Knox).

Frank Ramirez has served as a pastor for nearly 30 years in Church of the Brethren congregations in Los Angeles, California; Elkhart, Indiana; and Everett, Pennsylvania. A graduate of LaVerne College and Bethany Theological Seminary, Ramirez is the author of numerous books, articles, and short stories. His CSS titles include *Breakdown on Bethlehem Street*, *Partners in Healing*, *He Took a Towel*, *The Bee Attitudes*, and three volumes of *Lectionary Worship Aids*.

Argile Smith is Vice President for Advancement at William Carey University in Hattiesburg, Mississippi. He previously served at New Orleans Baptist Theological Seminary (NOBTS) as a preaching professor, chairman of the Division of Pastoral Ministries, and director of the communications center. While at NOTBS, Smith regularly hosted the Gateway to Truth program on the FamilyNet television network. He has also been the pastor of several congregations in Louisiana and Mississippi. Smith's articles have been widely published in church periodicals, and he is the author or editor of four books.

Peter Andrew Smith is an ordained minister in the United Church of Canada, currently serving St. James United Church in Antigonish, Nova Scotia. He is the author of *All Things Are Ready* (CSS), a book of lectionary-based communion prayers. He is also the author of a number of stories and articles, which can be found listed at www.peterandrewsmith.com.

The Rt. Rev. John S. Smylie, Bishop of Wyoming, previously served as the rector of St. Mark's Episcopal Church in Casper, Wyoming, and as the dean of the Cathedral of St. John the Evangelist in Spokane, Washington. He is a published author and storyteller as well as a singer-songwriter. Smylie recently completed *Grace for Today*, a collection of 25 stories that explores how grace, loss, and restoration are part of the same fabric.

www.ingramcontent.com/pod-product-compliance
Lightning Source LLC
Chambersburg PA
CBHW072015060426
42446CB00043B/2550